The Essential Writer's Guide — from the HillTop

Other books by the author

1. Pearls of Wisdom
2. Nuggets For Victorious Living
3. Stories To Warm Your Heart
4. Wisdom, Faith And A Song
5. They Touched Us For Good
6. Musings From The HillTop
7. All Things Bright And Beautiful
8. From Subri Anafoɔ To Pepease And Dansoman
9. Crossing The Bar—The Story of Daniel Opong Amoafo (DO)
10. Memoirs From The HillTop
11. Timeless Wisdom From The HillTop
12. Conversations From The HillTop
13. Counsels from The HillTop
14. Living With Purpose—HillTop Perspectives
15. Gems From The HillTop
16. Become An Investor! Not a Taker—HillTop Secrets

ENDORSEMENTS

Kofi Otutu Adu Labi's *The Essential Writer's Guide – from the HillTop* is not a manual in the narrow sense; it is a challenge to complacency. He reminds us that writing is not a pastime for elites but a discipline of permanence, a civic duty to record, to provoke, and to liberate. Too often, our societies underestimate the power of words, leaving stories trapped in silence. Adu Labi insists that discipline, routine, and courage are the antidotes to procrastination and self-doubt. His conversational style disarms, but beneath it lies a demand for seriousness: that writers become custodians of memory and agents of hope. He strips away mystification and insists that writing is about legacy, not vanity; about people, not performance. In a continent where imagination must be weaponised for renewal, this book is a timely provocation. It calls us to write as if lives depend on it—because they do.

Yaw Nsarkoh
Thinker
An African of the soil and of the blood
Former Executive Vice-President of Unilever

Kofi's book is a heartfelt and practical guide for anyone aspiring to tell their story. Drawing from his decades of writing experience and rich life anecdotes, he demystifies the writing process—from overcoming procrastination to crafting engaging narratives—with warmth and clarity. His conversational style feels like a trusted friend sharing wisdom, making even the most daunting writing tasks approachable.

What truly sets this book apart is its universal appeal to all writing enthusiasts: it doesn't just teach skills, but instils order in the chaotic process of creating, and refines techniques that turn scattered thoughts into coherent prose. Most importantly, Kofi encourages readers to embrace authenticity—guiding them to weave their true feelings, reflections, and life experiences into a book that feels genuine, personal, and resonant. Whether you are dreaming of penning memoirs or honing your creative voice, this book equips you with actionable steps and encouragement to turn your ideas into tangible, meaningful work. It's a must-read for budding writers ready to embark on their literary journey.

Jeremy Lee Guan San
Business Owner
Malaysia

The Chinese translation of the above

科菲的这本书是一本衷心且实用的指南，适合任何渴望讲述自己故事的人。他凭借自己数十年的写作经验和丰富的人生轶事，以温暖和清晰的方式揭开了写作过程的神秘面纱——从克服拖延症到创作引人入胜的叙事。他对话式的风格就像一位值得信赖的朋友在分享智慧，使即使是最令人生畏的写作任务也变得平易近人。

这本书真正的独特之处在于它对所有写作爱好者的普遍吸引力：它不仅仅是教授技能，而且还在混乱的创作过程中建立秩序，并改进将零散的想法转化为连贯散文的技巧。最重要的是，科菲鼓励读者拥抱真实性——引导他们将真实的感受、思考和生活经历融入到一本书中，使其感觉真实、个性化且能引起共鸣。无论您是梦想撰写回忆录还是磨练您的创作声音，本书都为您提供了可操作的步骤和鼓励，将您的想法转化为有形的、有意义的作品。对于准备开始文学之旅的新兴作家来说，这是一本必读之作。

杰里米. 吕元山
马来西亚
商人
（来自美国哈该学院的同学）

This is a remarkable book that transports us to three distinct realms: the world of the successful writer, the world of the expectant reader, and the world that awaits the generation in an AI-driven landscape—a vacuum, denied of shared authentic lived experiences that needed to be documented—lacking depth only because we would not.

This book is not just a self-help nonfiction guide; it is a call to action written in Kofi's unique storytelling and conversational manner. He goes beyond the instructional and invites other voices to confirm that indeed writing matters: it inspires; it entertains; it educates; and it guides. The abrupt ending, the writer's subtle conversational persuasive technique, immediately evokes the need to drop the book, pull out our drafts or the manuscripts "in our heads" and get started!

Vera Ekuwa Mansa Arhin, PhD
Founder and CEO, Educase Literacy Consult

This book attests to the adage that there is no success without a successor. The book contains practical gems of wisdom to embolden the ordinary person to dare to be a seasoned writer.

Rev. Dr Emmanuel Kwabena Ansah
Pastor, Church Governance Advisor & Author
Executive Director, Kingdom Equip Network

This book takes you on a friendly journey of the A to Z of writing in a way that will leave you speechless on how so much can be obtained in one book on writing and make you eager to read what is about to unfold in the next paragraph.

The Elegance of this book is in its simplicity. The ebbs and flow of the information is harmonious.

The book is free-flowing and whets the appetite of a budding writer who wants to take writing very seriously.

The author indeed speaks from the pinnacle of understanding of how to be a writer and this appeals to the inner cravings of a novice who is yearning to be a writer. I recommend this book to all who are pregnant with a story.

Dr Jerry Coleman
Consultant Obstetrician Gynaecologist and Head of the Maternal Fetal Medicine Unit, Korle-Bu Teaching Hospital, Accra, Ghana
Member, Editorial Board of the International Journal of Obstetrics and Gynaecology. Associate Editor in charge of Africa and East Mediterranean

After writing sixteen interesting, life-changing non-fiction and entertaining books, the author has graciously served his readers a delightful menu on the A-Z of writing. As I read the manuscript, I was reminded of Habakkuk 2:2 in the Bible:

"And the LORD answered me, and said: 'Write the vision, and make it plain upon tables, that he may run that readeth it'" (KJV).

Here is a written vision, and whoever reads it has a number of options, including running and acting on the guidelines, reading it very fast or slowly and getting on with one's own writing project.

The first time I heard the author speak on 'writing', he advised that one should always have a small note pad and pen on hand for capturing whatever great learning point that comes up. After reading this very enlightening book, I feel energised and ready to embark on my own writing journey. Thank you for this very helpful book on how to achieve one's writing dream, Kofi Otutu Adu Labi.

HE Abigail Naa Adzoko Kwashi
Ambassador of Ghana to the Kingdom of Norway, Republic of Finland and Republic of Iceland
Children's Service Teacher of the Presbyterian Church of Ghana

It's a real honour to comment on Lawyer Kofi Otutu Adu Labi's latest book *The Essential Writer's Guide—from the HillTop*.

For someone with such a full career, it's a marvel he has the time to produce as many publications as seventeen books and counting. So Kofi Adu Labi may be just the best person to give sound advice about how to write.

The book draws on the writer's rich and diverse professional and civic experience to offer insightful and practical advice about the writing process. He establishes the positive correlation between reading and writing, intimating he was a voracious reader growing up. That may account for his multiple wins in the ever-popular national "What Do You Know?" radio quiz competition.

If you want to be a writer—and a great one at that—you must read, says Kofi Adu Labi.

Raymond Tuvi
Media and Development Consultant

Writing is indeed a powerful medium of communication and this has been amply demonstrated by the author in this very readable, educative and exciting book.

I classify this *Essential Writer's Guide* by Kofi Otutu Adu Labi as a contemporary Golden Toolkit which transcends generations. He identifies the hurdles, misconceptions and successes of writing and addresses them so beautifully and persuasively.

The author is an ambidextrous and extraordinary writer who has endeared himself to his readers as a community leader who brings his people running to the baobab tree for storytelling.

Kofi has demystified the "Born Before Computer" (BBC) syndrome to your "Best Bet is the Computer" (BBITC). He emphasises visibility on New Media which has huge benefits for a successful writer both at home and abroad.

I doff my hat to you, the Multifaceted one!

Ayekooooo.

Cornelia Amoah
Broadcast Journalist and author of Women of Distinction Ghana: Journey to the Top—the book that celebrates 50 distinguished Ghanaian women in various disciplines

The Essential Writer's Guide—from the Hilltop is an enjoyable read that addresses the challenge of aspiring writers having low motivation or self-doubt in beginning their writing journey. It walks readers through the processes of generating ideas from everyday observations and insights, to putting down their first thoughts even when it makes little sense, to finally proofreading over and over until it makes a coherent piece.

What makes the book even more enjoyable is that it draws some of its insights from the Bible which reinforces the themes of discipline, patience, purpose, and so much more. Reading this ingenious piece should leave you feeling more motivated, encouraged, and guided to not only start writing, but complete it with a renewed confidence and a clarified mind.

Allswell Kosima Abankwa
Head, Climate and Sustainability Office
Bank of Ghana

I have read the book thoroughly and appreciate its content highly. It is a timely intervention for aspiring fiction or non-fiction writers as well as an inspiration for veteran writers. Once upon a time, I was an aspiring writer, who would have gained tremendous guidance from this Guidebook. I wrote sporadically, without the strict discipline that this Guidebook teaches. I learnt some of the disciplines of writing that are portrayed vividly in this manuscript whilst I wrote, sometimes in frustration.

A guidebook like this would have certainly allayed my fears and calmed my nerves. This book provides hands-on guidance from the outset and answers the questions that aspiring writers may have, particularly those that prevent them from reaching their goal of becoming writers. As an author of nine Christian non-fiction books, I endorse this Guidebook as a tool and ammunition for aspiring and ardent writers.

Rosemond Opare-Kumi (Dr Kumi)
Lecturer, Gaborone University College
Botswana, Broadhurst Campus, Gaborone

The Essential Writer's Guide—from the HillTop by Kofi Otutu Adu Labi is a thoughtfully crafted resource designed to inspire and support aspiring writers. With his extensive experience as a prolific author of 16 books, Adu Labi brings a wealth of expertise and passion to this engaging guide. The book features focused, linked lessons crafted to make the writing process accessible and motivating. Every effort has been made to create an interactive approach that encourages creativity, critical thinking, and confidence in writing.

Whether exploring storytelling, composition, or editing, this guide provides practical advice, inspiring prompts, and structured exercises to nurture a deep love for writing. Adu Labi's dedication to fostering the art of writing makes this an essential tool for anyone eager to develop their voice and skills, 'from the HillTop to the wider world beyond.'

Francis Gbormittah, PhD
Department of Theatre Arts
School of Performing Arts, University of Ghana

I have always wanted to be a writer, but there were no teachers. Finally, my problem has been solved with this very useful and insightful Guide.

I consider it a privilege to have been asked by the author to read this book in advance of publication. I have found it to be a very useful and loving Guide to prospective writers. As I read it, I realised I have books in my mind which I need to give birth to. This book has increased my knowledge about what it takes to write a book. I have learnt how to be more useful to society through the ministry of writing and sharing what I have been given by God. In the process, I have also got to know a bit more of Kofi's heart, wisdom and inspiration for living.

I pray the Lord empowers him and enlarges his boundaries as he continues to share Kingdom values and principles.

This book has been a blessing to me. I recommend it strongly.

Ricardo Mauro de Abreu
Pastor President @ Vida Com Cristo Vitória and
CEO @ Rima Business Brasil

This book catches the attention of the reader by just the title.

The tone of the author is encouraging and inclusive, aiming to reach readers from diverse backgrounds who wish to embark on their writing journey.

The book is well-organised, with chapters covering the motivations for writing, styles, building blocks, creativity, discipline, practical steps, and the absolute importance of reading for all seeking to become writers.

As with the author's earlier books, the writing style is conversational, simple, and engaging, making complex ideas accessible to a broad audience. In fact, it is like having a captivating engagement in person with the writer.

I encourage every aspiring writer to dig deep into it to get practical guidance to achieve their goal of becoming a writer. This book is a great resource that will help make your dream of becoming a writer come true.

Justice (Mrs) Afia Serwah Asare-Botwe (JA)
Court of Appeal, Ghana

I have always wanted to write!!! However, where to begin from, and how to weave and construct all the lovely mental pictures in my mind into a book, was simply a daunting and near impossible task.

For people like me who want to write but do not know how to proceed, this book could not have come at a better time.

Mr Kofi Otutu Adu Labi, a prolific author, begins with the question, "Why write at all?" and leads the reader through varied reasons why one should write. He also leads the reader through some writing styles and gently guides with some "Building Blocks" for effective writing.

It is an honour for me to be associated with this book, and I have no reason not to come out with my first book, after the inspiration I have received from this gem of a book.

Rev. Ebenezer Kofi Adeyemi Decker
District Minister, Presbyterian Church of Ghana,
Fafraha

THE ESSENTIAL WRITER'S GUIDE – FROM THE HILLTOP

Kofi Otutu Adu Labi

THE ESSENTIAL WRITER'S GUIDE — FROM THE HILLTOP

ISBN: 978-9988-41-704-8

For copies and other enquiries, contact the author through
ksenior51@gmail.com

Cover design and page layout by Sam Nyarko-Mensah

CONTENTS

to

my readers and cheerleaders, home and abroad, whose never-ceasing messages of encouragement have inspired me to produce this Writer's Guide. This is a token of my appreciation to you. Be inspired to embark on your own writing journeys.

ACKNOWLEDGEMENTS

All praise and thanks to God for the gift of life and the ability to keep on writing. This is my seventeenth book and I am full of wonder and praise to the Lord for seeing me through this.

Writing a book is a complete project whose success depends considerably on the support of others. I have benefitted greatly from insights and editorial assistance from the following who gave of their time to read the manuscript and offer me invaluable advice.

These are my son-in-law Kwao Aidoo, and my friends Mrs Elizabeth Frimpomah Frimpong and Mrs Josephine Osafo-Affum. They drew my attention to some otherwise obvious editorial matters needing correction which had escaped my tired eyes. I am also grateful to Rev. Dr Emmanuel Kwabena Ansah for some very good editorial comments.

Sam Nyarko-Mensah has been with me right from the beginning, right from the publication of my first three books, *Stories to Warm your Heart, Pearls of Wisdom* and *Nuggets for Victorious Living*. Though he has left Step Publishers to pursue doctoral studies abroad, he still made time to provide the usual services and advice that would lead to a successful transition from manuscript to book release.

I am particularly grateful to Professor Akosua Adomako Ampofo, distinguished international scholar, for her thought-provoking Foreword. I also owe a debt of gratitude to the eminent panel of Endorsers who took the trouble to read the manuscript before proceeding to write the statements of praise which give a feel of what the reader is to expect before starting to read the book.

As usual, I am grateful to my wife Elioenai, children and in-laws for the various acts of support which have helped to make this book a reality.

To God be the glory.

FOREWORD

As someone who writes for a living (academics are paid to not only teach, but also to do research and to publish their findings), I cannot overstate the importance of clear, concise, interesting and edifying writing as a tool, both for informing as well as encouraging the reader. We live in precarious and troubling times, and too often, information is presented as essential-for-you-to-know, while it is merely curated in ways that exhaust with news about wars, and anger you with tales of injustice, or worse, deplete you of hope because you cannot envision an end in sight. Some writing is also just downright bad—poor grammar, unwieldy sentences, disconnected thoughts, repetitions, devoid of sign posting to guide the reader from one topic to another, and boring!

Writing—whether fiction, auto/biographical, news, or documentary, can generate hope for our times through the details that are shared, and importantly, how they are shared. The stories must come alive, we must experience the context and feel with the protagonists; achieving this requires passion, commitment, and of course skill. While I am of the school of thought that some are born writers, just as some are born athletes, I also believe that passion, commitment, and skill can be learned and nurtured. This is what *The Essential Writer's Guide—from the HillTop* by Kofi Otutu Adu Labi seeks to do. He is himself a prolific author—having 16 books to his credit, most written from the "hill top"; no doubt, where the serene, green environment provides ideal conditions for reflection and writing undisturbed by the sights, sounds and smells of the urbanscape. He is also a sought-after speaker, which is often an indication of a person's writing prowess.

Writing is both an art and a science. By that I mean that writing has a particular technical format, style and strategies to accomplish the writing task. At the same time, the writer needs to be able to anticipate readers' needs, be responsive to changes in reading cultures, and meet readers' yearnings through the page. Some people are able to combine these skills in their writings. However, just like not every Professor of quantum physics is necessarily able to deftly explain the complexities of how the universe behaves for people to understand and enjoy, not every author can necessarily convey the how-to-become-a-writer to aspiring authors.

In your hands you hold a book designed to simplify the journey of putting together a piece of writing for the budding author. In *The Essential Writer's Guide—from the HillTop*, Kofi Otutu Adu Labi breaks down the basic ingredients and how-tos of writing in a simple, engaging and straightforward style. It was interesting for me, as a writer myself, to see how many of these I practised, some consciously, others less so. I found myself nodding, smiling, remembering struggles that could have been avoided had someone taught me some of these basics long ago.

I laughed hard when I read about producing books in the head (Ch. 1), as this was me, until I began the practice of always having a notebook in my bag or by my bedisde to capture experiences, creative phrases and other reflections. Failing that, I just drop some written or voice notes on my phone. There are those authors who feel that creative writing is only for fiction, and so the poor reader has to plod through pages of boring details. In chapter 2, we find tips on how a writer can make even 'factual' writing interesting—this was the difference between my own seconday school Form 2 and Form 3 French teachers. The former made the language come alive, the latter offered a boring, arduous journey through grammar, syntax and vocabulary. I blame her for the fact that I dropped French and did not take it to my 'O' Levels.

Creating suspense and a sense of adventure is as important for fiction as for non-fiction. These themes continue in chapters 3 and 4, with practical tips on how to evoke imagery, while also buckling down to the hard discipline of a structured routine. Every struggling writer will be reassured when they get to chapter 5, if they are not already, when they read, "Don't pay too much attention to the initial nonsense you write". We learn that every piece of writing is a raw draft that can be refined later. This is so true, and when I look at my own writing, I sometimes find that I have more than 10 versions. Even the early "nonsense" ones sometimes contain gems which, though they didn't make it into the final book, chapter, article or blog, years later earn a place in another publication. Skip to chapter 7 and the sage advice is offered to know your audience. The fact that we have something to say doesn't mean everyone wants to hear or read it; as they say, "Read the room". When we look at the preaching of Jesus Christ, we can see that He tailored his words to his audience, using familiar anecdotes and parables to engender authentic connection. There are other nuggets in *The Essential Writer's Guide*: finding cheerleaders who will offer constructive criticism; reading what you wrote out loud; putting the work away for a time lest you miss the forest for the trees; the importance of being a prolific reader if you want to be a good writer. *The Essential Writer's Guide* even provides a template for the structure of a book (Ch. 14).

I am really pleased that this simple, practical and interesting how-to guide is available for budding, and even well-known authors. Whether you are a writer of creative fiction, non-fiction, news stories, blogs or academic pieces, this should be essential reading.

Professor Emerita Akosua Adomako Ampofo
Centre for Gender Studies and Advocacy
University of Ghana
Fellow of the Ghana Academy of Arts and Sciences

INTRODUCTION

The never-ending questions about writing that keep coming to me from all sections of the reading public never cease to amaze me. A deep-seated desire on the part of many people to become writers emerges all the time. It is clear that many are those who aspire to be writers but feel constrained by thoughts of inadequacy or even ignorance. Some have a mental picture of what they wish to share with the world through writing. Their difficulty, however, is with how to translate the contents of the mental pictures into tangible material into book form.

This book is therefore designed to offer help and guidance to demystify the book writing process and to free budding writers from whatever is preventing them from maximising their writing potential.

Having already authored sixteen other books and contributed a chapter to a book co-authored by two other authors, there are many experiences, lessons and best practices I have picked up along the way which will undoubtedly be useful to aspiring writers. This is my motivation for this latest publication from my "HillTop Writing Academy" which I have aptly titled *The Essential Writer's Guide—from the HillTop*. I pray that you will be inspired and empowered to embark on your writing journey after reading, and re-reading this book.

The plain truth is that writing is a process, call it journey if you wish, demanding patience, perseverance, focus, open-mindedness and above all, discipline. When all these, and others you will come across either directly or by implication, come into play, you will in the course of time reach that dream destination of not only holding a book of your own in your hands, but more importantly, a book you can be sure will enrich the lives of those who read it and be a legacy after you.

1

WHY WRITE AT ALL?

"A room without books is like a body without a soul." – Marcus Tullius Cicero

For the art of writing to become meaningful, it is critical to appreciate its place in the shaping of history. Writing can never be in a vacuum and such an understanding gives authenticity to it.

Writing provides permanence

Writing is very much a part of human civilisation, so said a speaker at the Haggai Institute for Advanced Leadership on the beautiful island of Maui in Hawaii in August 2008. The statement is true!

Among other qualities, good writing gives permanence, removes ambiguity and provides authenticity to ideas and themes. Writing confirms, informs, teaches and encourages the reader. I have no doubt that we can all identify with these attributes of writing. Why then do some of us find it so difficult to put anything down in writing? The things you write will still be speaking to the reader long after you are dead and gone.

A good aspiration

This is something good to aspire to. Literally everyone I meet who has read one or more of my books or even when they have not but get to know that I am a writer tells me they want to become writers. I take it that my being a writer is what makes them feel comfortable in approaching me. Hardly a week goes by without one person or the other approaching me, especially at church and functions, and posing questions to me on the art of writing. Many desire to be writers and to release their own books. What a laudable objective! If this describes you, take heart. There is hope.

Let's do this together

I am convinced that we can work together, through this little book, to help you attain your objective. What is needed is an open mind and a willingness to recognise the pitfalls along the way and in the process follow the examples of those who have established a track record in the area of writing. Why suffer needlessly when you can learn best practice from the struggles and successes of others? Why reinvent the wheel when you can learn from what others have gone through?

Are you producing books in your head?

Many are those who have written books upon books in their heads. You read right. Yes, I have heard and witnessed this trend at work over and over. Books written in the minds of people. Unbelievable, but true and funny. At a book launch I attended in Accra in late 2022, I could barely contain my laughter listening to two guest speakers at the function lament, while congratulating the author, about their inability to transfer, as it were, the "books in their heads" into real books that could be read by the world. One of the guest speakers had already written three books in her head and the other five in his head. I also remember with amusement the day a colleague of mine in congratulating me on my books, said something to the effect that: "You have done well, Kofi. My problem is how to get all the lofty ideas in my head into a format for a book."

Why have you not written that book?

On the other side of the spectrum are those who just underestimate what it takes to be a writer and think that they can just decide to write and author books at any time. I got into conversation with a professional colleague I had not met in a long time at a public event. She congratulated me on my book writing and went on to make a remark many who do not understand the dynamics of writing often make to a writer. The lady, to paraphrase her, said, Oh, it is not surprising that you have written all these books, with so much time on your hands because you are no longer involved in full-time work. Really, I asked myself, do you know what you are talking about? To her credit, this colleague lady lawyer friend of mine, also on partial retirement, then turned round some moments later and asked herself why she had not written a single book since she was no longer in full-time employment if it were that easy to write books.

There is no magic wand

The hard to accept fact, by those who lack appreciation of what is involved in writing, is that if writing books were so easy, bookshelves at home and in bookshops would be overflowing with books.

Oh dear! Who will deliver these budding writers, young and old, from their inability to transform their dreams into reality? My simple answer is that there is no magic wand to wave or special tricks involved, just some tried and tested practical steps I have experienced over the years. Come along with me as we explore, share and learn from these practical steps borne out of experiences in authoring books as well as sharing daily messages to a global audience on social networks like Linkedln and Facebook.

2

WRITING STYLES

"What is the essence of the art of writing? Part One: Have something to say. Part Two: Say it well." – Edward Abbey, American author and essayist.

As a writer, be clear about the approach to adopt in your writing. You cannot be all things to everyone and knowing your style will help you in disseminating your message effectively.

I write creative non-fiction

I must make it clear that the genre I apply is creative non-fiction. As a creative writer, the one thing that started me on the journey and has kept me going is the realisation that I have a story to tell. People like stories and a good story is an avenue to send across a message and a lesson. Every writer is a missionary. You tell your stories through your writings.

Whatever you write, whether as an essay, short article or especially a book, will only be useful to the world if read. It is therefore of utmost importance that we make a conscious effort to come to terms with the dynamics of writing for it to become an instrument of change, for the good of the reader and the society at large.

I have come to appreciate a number of writing styles which help to engage the interest of the reader. A key one, for me, is storytelling which has become the hallmark of most of my writings.

Stories are powerful

Stories are a pleasurable way to get people to remember things. Stories are a powerful medium of communication and storytelling enhances the appeal of all genres.

Storytelling engages the reader, and in this connection you need to remember that writing is about engaging the reader. In what ways can you engage your reader, I hear you asking?

Use Stories

Your daily experiences become stories and anecdotes, and they can deliver an important message as easily as they can make your audience laugh or cry. This is a style I have kept on using. If you apply the power of observation, you will not fail to notice otherwise mundane things in your surroundings which you can turn into stories with accompanying lessons. All my books apply storytelling as a way of illustrating a point, drawing out lessons and sharing values I deem important.

Without exception, my readers and audiences have always responded enthusiastically to real life stories as they almost always find themselves relating to them. I remember one story based on an experience in Rio de Janeiro in Brazil that I shared in my book, *Memoirs from the HillTop*. The story always gets readers reacting with joy. One reader even made a point of calling me from his base in the United States of America one early morning when he got to that point in the book. We both went into bouts of giggling as we went over the story again.

Stories can draw your audience into your life and allow them to see, hear, touch, taste and smell what was going on around you when you were in another geographical location.

Stories and anecdotes will draw your audience closer to you and allow you to engage with them much easier.

People love stories. Readers easily engage with stories. They find them enjoyable and remember them too. Jesus was a storyteller. Who does not remember the various parables He narrated? *The Parable of the Good Samaritan* is one example.

The Parable of the Good Samaritan, found in Luke 10:25-37, tells the story of a traveller who is robbed, beaten, and left for dead on the side of the road. A priest and a Levite, both figures of religious importance, pass by without offering assistance. A Samaritan, a member of a group traditionally despised by Jews, stops to help the injured man, bandaging his wounds, taking him to an inn, and paying for his care.

The parable emphasises that true neighbourly love extends to everyone, even those considered enemies or outsiders.

The Parable of the Prodigal Son is another example of good storytelling by Jesus, leaving unforgettable lessons for hearers then and now.

The Parable of the Prodigal Son, found in Luke 15:11-32, tells the story of a son who asks for and receives his inheritance early, then squanders it on reckless living. After falling into poverty, he returns home, expecting to be a servant, but his father welcomes him back with open arms and a celebration. This parable highlights themes of forgiveness, redemption, and God's unconditional love.

Speaking for myself, I can recommend the following attributes of good writing:

Simplicity—I have come to accept that simplicity is a powerful tool to apply in writing. It helps readers to be motivated to continue reading your book instead of putting it away after reading the first few pages. It makes them feel comfortable with what you are sharing. I must say that readers without count have commented on the simplicity of my writing style and added that they have become loyal readers of mine as a result.

A conversational style

A conversational style of writing keeps the reader engaged and immersed in what you have written. Again, this is a style I apply in my writings and I see that it gets readers absorbed in them. In her statement of endorsement to my book *Musings from the HillTop*, Ambassador Esther Dzifa Ofori states among other things that, "In flawless conversational English, the writer takes you through different chapters of his life which he freely shares with his readers."

Passion

The passion with which you write should infect your reader with a desire to stay with you to the end. One particular reader, a surgeon based in the United Kingdom, in commenting on my *Memoirs from the HillTop* wrote about how I manage to hold the unsuspecting reader captive by the sheer thrill of the narration.

Suspense

Write in such a way that your readers will always want to turn to the next page and chapter to read what is coming next. One of the joys of my writing experience has been to receive telephone calls from near and far from readers telling me that they were still awake reading a book of mine well beyond their bedtimes. Someone even posted an image of one of my books (*Pearls of Wisdom*) on Facebook on one occasion, saying that he just could not put it down even though it was almost midnight and he knew he had to be up early the next day to leave for an assignment.

On other occasions while serialising stories on social media, I have had readers contacting me privately and pleading that I tell them what had been promised in the next instalment, saying they could not wait till the next day! Of course, I always responded calmly, asking them to be patient.

3

THE BUILDING BLOCKS

"There is no greater agony than bearing an untold story inside you." – Maya Angelou (I Know Why the Caged Bird Sings)

A very helpful approach in writing is for the writer to start from basics in terms of the foundations, of ideas and context, to carry the reader along right from the onset.

Keep imagery alive

Use imagery, through words and sentences which describe places and events you are writing about. The way you describe events as they unfold, be it in fiction or non-fiction, will keep the reader glued to what you have written.

At this juncture let me share one example of what I mean by keeping imagery alive. It is an excerpt from my book *Wisdom, Faith and a Song*, while describing my visit to the American Protestant Church in The Hague in the year 2014. Here we go.

The service was an inspiring one, with the resident minister dwelling on the importance of keeping true to one's covenant relationship.

The singing by the visiting American male voice choir was glorious. To begin with, they numbered about 30 in all and they all wore cream coats over black attires and had cream bow ties. They were mostly in their sixties, and I guessed that they were all retirees, like me. The conductor, however, was in a black suit. It was clear that each member of the choir was passionate about what he was doing.

There was also a certain air of joy and enthusiasm flowing from the conductor. It was obvious that the members of the choir had their eyes trained on him, waiting for his signal. From the moment he beckoned to them to get up from their seats to get ready to sing, one could feel the expectancy emanating from the congregation. The conductor lifted his right hand to conduct, and the music that flowed from the choir at that command filled the church with unspeakable joy. Among the songs they sang was, "Crown Him with many crowns . . ."

You could hear a pin drop! It was so moving. It was so sweet. It was so exhilarating. They sang with all their heart and all their strength. The lyrics came out of their throats at full throttle. It was as if the angels in heaven had come down. In Ghana we would say, when we have such an experience that, "*Nyame yɛ dɛ*, the literal translation of which is "God is sweet", but whose right interpretation should be, "It is a great thing to serve the Lord."

I have been to countries I have still not visited in person and experienced events at which I was not physically present through the powerful imagery embodied in words and sentences in books I read during my younger years.

Creating content

Every interaction gives rise to writing ideas.

You will find that as you pay attention to your surroundings and the people you are interacting with, writing ideas will come to you that you can develop into stories. Sometimes someone will ask a question or make a comment and almost immediately an idea will come to you which you can develop into a storyline.

People sometimes wonder how I create stories out of otherwise mundane things and situations. I have a standard response and recommendation on this matter. To create content, make it a habit to move beyond just looking at things. There is almost always a story and application from every situation or scene. You will see the story or lesson if you make it a point to see, and not just look. This is akin to people sitting on wealth in the form of natural resources and yet living in poverty because they have not cultivated their powers of observation and discernment. Don't we see this all the time, especially in our part of the world? Look, and see, and dig up the gems you are sitting on and translate them into stories and opportunities.

Indeed, most of the storytelling I have been applying in my books and writings and which my readers have found so enjoyable, have come about because of observations I made while at a location or function and also while interacting with people. Oftentimes, I have had people telling me after reading what I wrote, "Oh, that didn't occur to me but looking back it was so obvious!"

Rebuild ideas you pick up with your own understanding

The world is overflowing with ideas and they are accessible in print and especially on social media. Many of these ideas have positive and promising indicators, even if they have not been acted upon. The creative mind in you should encourage you to pick some of these ideas, rebuild them with your worldview and share them in your writings. No one has a monopoly of ideas. The truth is that quite often originality comes from mixing things already in existence. So feel emboldened to study ideas you come across and deconstruct and model them to fit your storyline.

Take notes

I have always insisted that the shortest pencil is superior to the longest memory. It is Richard Branson who said: "If you don't write your ideas down, they could leave your head before you even leave the room." For as long as I can remember, I have been taking notes at whatever function I attend. To this end, I always carry a notepad or diary and pen with me. I have often been amazed at myself whenever I have gone back to notes captured while attending functions. The notes jotted down have often proved to be invaluable context and content for my writings.

Keep hope alive

If you want to be a writer readers will take seriously, let what you write bring hope to them. Many are those weighed down by burdens of different shapes. You should structure your writing to give hope to your readers. You do so by sharing experiences from your life and elsewhere of how you, and others, were able to face and overcome obstacles, in some cases overwhelming ones.

Sound genuine

Never forget that writing is a powerful medium with which to reach and influence people for good.

Your primary motivation should be to share things with the world that will increase, and not decrease, it. This implies that you should write in an area you have a conviction in.

For example, my *Memoirs from the HillTop* is a deliberate attempt to share lessons from my life and in the process give direction and encouragement to both the young and old in navigating the different stages of life. I share a couple of unpalatable details about myself which, based on feedback from some readers, have made the book authentic and credible.

Your motivation will therefore not to make money but rather to leave a legacy of impact. The money may well come as a by-product of your dedication to writing but should not be the motivation.

4

WRITING IS CREATIVITY

"And by the way, everything in life is writable about if you have the outgoing guts to do it, and the imagination to improvise. The worst enemy to creativity is self-doubt." – Sylvia Plath (The Unabridged Journals of Sylvia Plath)

The effort involved in writing should not be underestimated. Pay attention to the underlying factors and you will get it right.

Writing is problem-solving

People are looking for solutions to problems they are facing in life. Many are those who are hurting. I know this as a fact from the School of Life. Things are not always what they appear to be.

Writing is a ministry that can offer much needed solutions through stories and perspectives shared by the author. In my writing experience, I have been inspired to hear people tell me that something

I wrote about or an experience I shared had been the answer to a problem or situation they had been grappling with. Others have testified about how my writings have been the enabling factor which led them to persevere and complete projects that had long delayed and seemed impossible to bring to conclusion. I am certain that other writers have similar stories to share.

This is one more reason why you should aspire to be a writer.

Writing takes discipline

You underestimate this to your undoing. Writing is very hard work. Let me drum that into you. Discipline is something you need to practise as a way of life if you want to achieve anything you set your mind to. You need to be disciplined in your use of time. You need to watch out for the time wasters. They could be legitimate in every sense but in reality an enemy to your aspirations. A busy day is not the same as a productive day. Immersing yourself in things that do not advance your priorities will not only leave you exhausted but despairing of not making progress with your writing project. You will end up making excuses and ascribing the blame to others, when the culprit is the person you see in the mirror, yourself.

Daily practice is key

I cannot emphasise this enough. If you want to be a writer, you have to develop the habit of writing day after day after day. You may choose to call it routine, but I have always insisted that you need routine in your daily habits to become significant. This is an aspect of discipline which needs to be taken seriously. You are what you do repeatedly.

Your daily schedule

What you choose to do every single day matters more than what you do once in a while.

Choose the time window that is best suited for your daily schedule. If you are a morning person like me, write in the morning. I find that blocking half an hour to a maximum one hour each morning to sit at my laptop is very beneficial in advancing my writing objectives. So set aside writing time and use that time to create something new.

The power of routine

Your motivation or even strong desire to write is not enough, without more. This is where routine comes in.

Routine gets the job done even when you are tired, bored, or distracted.

Make it a point to develop systems and processes for life or work, even with the most basic things. For example, my phone, wallet, car keys and some other personal items are always kept in the same place. I don't have to think about them or look for them when I need them. I can walk with my eyes closed to pick them up from where I put them.

I have a daily routine for almost everything. The less I have to think about what's next, the more I get done.

You cannot go wrong if you establish a routine in your life. You will become better organised. You will have peace of mind. You will be a composed person and you will be productive as you pursue your writing assignments.

5

PAY ATTENTION TO THESE

"My aim is to put down on paper what I see and what I feel in the best and simplest way." – Ernest Hemingway

Writing can be enjoyable if you have a humble attitude. Be prepared to go the whole hog.

Don't pay too much attention to the initial nonsense you write

It does not matter if what you write initially is utter nonsense, so to speak. The important thing is to write something every day. It is a raw draft that can be refined later. In my case, I do even not bother to edit what I have written at the initial stages. I just make sure that I don't get up from my desk and laptop without having written something, most of which may not amount to much in their raw state. Indeed, they are, more often nonsense.

That first sentence!

The secret from my HillTop Writing Academy is that once I have jotted something down, it becomes easier for me to go back to it much later and try to edit and bring sense out of it. This is because the most difficult part of writing is, in many ways, the first sentence. If you doubt this, decide to write something on any subject and see how it goes. It could be a tribute to a deceased family member or colleague, a congratulatory message for a brochure or an address to a gathering. You may find that getting the first line written could be a herculean and totally intimidating task which if not handled well could derail the whole exercise.

I have encountered people who told me that the mere thought of that first sentence to help them to complete a writing assignment made them feel unwell.

Yes, that first sentence is crucial.

Writing is a way of connecting with the world

Writing is powerful. It transcends time and space and allows you to communicate with, and influence, people in different parts of the world in ways you cannot even start to imagine.

As a writer you should therefore be curious, courageous, compassionate, and humble. These are traits that will enable you make the right observations about people, places and events and help make what you write more impactful.

Do not tell the world what you intend to do prematurely

This is one sure way of killing the dream. Premature optimism will kill what you plan to do. The psychological satisfaction you get from telling the world about the books in your head will prevent you, in practice, from sitting down to do the hard work of working on your writing project day after day with the rigour required. Important things need time to incubate before they burst on to the world stage.

Great writing does not just happen

The more you write, the better the chances of you becoming a better writer.

Write as often as you can. One or two paragraphs a day will eventually add up. Just do it. Did you take note? Just do it! The point cannot be overemphasised that consistency pays off!

See your writing as a calling

Once you see your writing as a calling or ministry, you will have the passion to keep going.

What you need is just one idea, an idea that will fuel your calling and ministry as a writer to leave the world a better place than you found it.

Manage your energy

This means directing your energy in the right direction, in this case towards your writing goals. In practical terms, this means being at peace with yourself and others. Peace makes a lot of difference to being a creative writer. When you are at peace with others, especially your family members, creativity will be released. Otherwise your adrenalin will be misdirected into unproductive, energy sapping and wasteful thoughts. This will in turn affect your health and prevent you from achieving your writing goals and they will become a pie in the sky.

Dedicate regular times to reading, studying and thinking

In this connection, periods spent in solitude can yield rich dividends. Solitude will help you to think through and incubate writing ideas.

Invest your time wisely. Don't just spend your time. Focus on effectiveness, not efficiency.

6

WRITING TIPS TO KEEP IN VIEW

"Write. Rewrite. When not writing or rewriting, read. I know of no shortcuts."
– Larry L. King

There are no shortcuts in writing and you need to understand this.

As a writer, you are unique

If you don't write that book, it will never be written. Writing is a process. You write a word, a sentence, a paragraph and then a chapter.

It is good to have subtitles. Give your readers eye breaks

I am conscious of this and employ this style in my writings. The result is that my readers find it a pleasurable experience reading my books and do not feel weary, as it were. You need a good lead for every chapter. The lead can make the reader want to continue reading. Also have a strong ending to every chapter, to encourage the reader to want to move on to the next one.

Write the way you speak. Seek to engage your reader

Ever so often, readers have told me that as they read my works, they feel as if they are sitting in front of me and we are having a conversation. This conversational style of writing keeps the reader fully engaged and absorbed with what they are reading.

Don't write with the aim of impressing with big words

Plain English makes your writing interesting and reader friendly.

Always use the simplest words, words that would keep your readers interested in your book. Long sentences may send the readers to sleep. Oh yes, they may find themselves sleeping without having taken a sleeping tablet.

There should be no clutter

Don't just try to fill the pages up and increase your word count. You could produce a boring book otherwise. Good writing is measured by what is taken out and not by how bulky the book is.

Double check your facts.

Let accuracy be the hallmark of your writing. If you are not sure of a date or the facts or details of something you are writing about, be diligent about crosschecking them. You have no excuse for not doing so. In any event, there are numerous avenues for doing so, be they technological, credible records or even from trusted and knowledgeable people.

How can you find time to write?

No one is going to give you time to write. We all have 24 hours in a day. This is true whether you are a President, Chief Executive Officer or the average person. You must make time to write. Find periods during the day, in the early morning or at the end of day. They can be slots of a few minutes at a time. They will add up eventually. You will have the time needed to write when you rearrange your priorities. You just must make the time to write, the same way lovers of say the English Premier League carve out time to follow their teams whenever they are playing a match. It is not about working longer hours. It is about being focused on the right hours.

A good habit is to use periods spent waiting for an appointment or at a hospital to see a doctor to continue working on whatever current manuscript you have. This is a better and more sensible use of time than spending precious minutes staring at others or at the ceiling. Waiting at the airport, undertaking a long journey by coach, train or air, can be a golden opportunity to put your time to good use by writing. Of course, you can use such periods reading too. I do so whenever I travel or have to wait to see the doctor.

Just write!

The first step is to write every day.

Set aside writing time and create something new.

If you start doing this, something will happen to you without your noticing at first. You will build a habit, and with that habit will come more content than you may be able to use. I can testify that I have lots of content literally tucked away in diaries and notebooks that could be the material for many more books if I want to keep releasing books.

Build that writing habit

When you write every day, you will not struggle for content. And more importantly, the quality of your writing will keep improving as you keep to that regular regimen.

Just make sure that you have a notebook or electronic device on you wherever you go so that you utilise every spare time. The word for you here is simple. Redeem the time and you will reach your destination of producing that dream book earlier than you could imagine. Don't look for blocks of hours or days. They may never come and will become a mirage you never reach.

The point I am making is that yes, people often say they don't have time. The reality is that you need to build discipline first. You don't need more hours.

You need the right hours. One focused hour beats five distracted ones.

Put the draft away and revisit after some time

When you finish a draft, it is good practice to put it away. The fact is that you cannot edit your work objectively during the writing process. Indeed, quite often your eyes may deceive you into overlooking otherwise obvious errors of spelling, grammar and punctuation. However, if you put it away and return to it at a later date, you will find that you are able to spot minor mistakes and edit or restructure appropriately. The result will be for you to be able to write subjectively and edit objectively.

In revisiting and rewriting this book for almost three years now, I always use the opportunity to improve on what I wrote earlier.

7

MAKING WHAT YOU WRITE STRIKE HOME

"Writing is an exploration. You start from nothing and learn as you go."
– E. L. Doctorow

It is always good to have a game plan and a roadmap when setting out on the writing journey. You will save yourself a lot of pain that way.

Know your audience

As a writer, you need to know your audience. Engage in serious self-evaluation along the following lines:

Start by identifying your target audience and understanding their needs, challenges, and aspirations. What questions do they have? What obstacles are they facing? How can your expertise help them achieve their goals?

Why are you writing? You write because you have a storyline and message for your reader. You don't write because someone you know has written a book and you also wish to be known as a writer and become known in society. That is a false and slippery start.

Seek out the "why" behind the "what" you are doing. You need to be honest with yourself. Your motivation will play a great role in your becoming a writer. You need to have an overriding desire to write. You need to have a story to share. You should not seek to become a writer because you are under the impression that it is a route to riches. You could get badly disappointed.

Who are you writing for? You write because there are people out there who are hurting and who will surely benefit from your experiences. They need to hear your story.

What are they looking for? Your readers are looking for answers. They are looking for inspiration. You must have an idea of the issues they are struggling with. What answers are they looking for?

What are you writing about? You must write about their everyday questions, trials, failures and struggles. They need to know that they are not alone in the struggles they are facing.

How do you intend to connect with your readers so they get your message? You must use examples and context they can relate to. Let what you write address the needs of your readers.

Write content that speaks directly to them using examples and stories they can relate to. Your writing will become more credible to them that way. By focusing on their fears, doubts and needs, your readers will come to see you as a trusted friend and expert whose views, as coming through in your book are authentic, reliable and trustworthy. You therefore need to bear in mind continuously that your book is playing the role of a consultant or even a medical doctor whose diagnosis and advice will help solve the problems and ailments of your readers and put them on a new pedestal.

Start with an outline, however sketchy

A big picture Outline with just the proposed key topics and events can provide direction for the way forward. Never forget that writing is a big journey and a potential destiny changer.

Setting off on the writing journey without a basic Outline may be likened to trying to build a house without a blueprint. I have seen many examples of this in my lifetime and have always felt sad for such projects, which invariably end up uncompleted or completed but lacking basic amenities. Sadly, some people do exactly that by just gathering workmen to the building site and delude themselves into thinking that they will get a satisfactory outcome. That will not give you a satisfactory outcome.

Start with an outline and be guided by it so you do not lose focus. Of course, you can make adjustments as you proceed with the writing process.

Adopt a GPS framework

Consider adopting a GPS framework, for want of a better terminology, for your writing blueprint. The digital age has come with many conveniences and driving to a previously unknown address, for example, is no longer the nightmare it used to be for some of us.

- G - Goals (What do you want your book to achieve? For you and for your reader?)
- P - Path (What journey will your reader take?)
- S - Steps (What steps are you going to take to make sure it happens?)

Having a clear plan makes a lot of difference. Once you have a clear plan, you have already set yourself up for turning your dream into reality.

Find your writing niche

The key is to write as if you are speaking to a friend. Your book should be engaging, conversational, and reflective of your unique personality and expertise. Be yourself and let your unique message come through. Your writing should let your voice be heard.

One way to develop your voice is to imagine that your ideal reader is sitting right in front of you, asking questions. How would you answer their questions? What would you say? Write what comes to mind. This exercise helps you tap into your natural writing style and overcome perfectionism.

Read what you write out loud

Another useful exercise is to read your writing out loud. Does it sound like something you would say in a conversation? If not, try *simplifying your language* or using more *relatable examples.* Remember, your readers want to feel like they are learning from a trusted friend or mentor, not someone out of touch with reality. Make it a habit to read to that person you see in the mirror every now and then. Obviously, that person in the mirror is you.

Focus on providing value to your readers

Your book should address their pain points, offer practical solutions, and share your unique insights and experiences. I still remember the evening I received a message through Facebook Messenger from someone in the United States of America telling me about how the messages in one of my books had proved to be such a blessing at a time she was going through some turbulent times. That initial communication opened the way for us to have very useful follow-up exchanges.

Write content that speaks directly to your reader. Use relatable examples, and stories to illustrate your points.

Your book is about your readers and the transformation you can help them achieve. Focus on their needs and provide answers and direction to their questions and needs. Create a book that resonates with your audience and positions you as a trusted expert in your field.

Improve on your writing skills

You can do this by contributing articles at various places, including church and community groups. This is something I do on a regular basis. The more you write, the better your writing becomes. This will set you apart from your peers and the likelihood of people wanting to read your books and other writings will be higher.

Determine the purpose of what you are writing

What result do you want to achieve? Are you looking to inform, persuade, or make a request? Let that purpose inform the substance and style of your communication from beginning to end.

In my case, my primary objective is to encourage, build up and inform the reader through the genre of storytelling using case studies where necessary. I have always sought to recommend best practice in terms of attitude, life skills and values that will have a positive impact on the reader.

Then, identify exactly who your audience is and speak directly to them

Always keep in mind that your writing is about the reader, not about you. This means using language that they understand and a voice that resonates with them. It also means anticipating and answering their questions — before they need to ask. Many are those looking for answers to troubling questions and issues confronting them.

Always make it a point to ask yourself, "What message am I trying to convey?"

This is the essential substance of your writing. If you want to be a writer, keep in mind that writing is not in a vacuum. Know that you are on a mission to inform, educate and to make society a better place. Indeed, writing is a powerful tool for social transformation.

Over the period that I have been writing, I have coined the term "the writer's glow" which describes the joy and sense of satisfaction that comes from knowing that lives are being touched for good through my writings. It's a very good feeling, I tell you. Thankfully, this is something I experience time and again. There have been occasions when complete strangers have walked up to me and told me that they had read a book or other writing of mine and had been blessed.

8

THE CASE FOR MEMOIRS

"I write for the same reason I breathe because if I didn't, I would die." – Isaac Asimov

You owe it to yourself and posterity to share lessons from your life. You never know who will benefit from them.

This is an area where we are now beginning to enjoy the benefits of the documented experiences of some of our achievers in society. There is still a lot more ground to be covered here, however, as many of our trailblazers are yet to write their stories. Many, sadly, have departed this life without telling their stories.

Memoirs share with your readers where you have come from, where you have been, what challenges you have faced and overcome and what lessons they can pick from your life so they do not have to reinvent the wheel. Memoirs share about your relationships and your achievements. Memoirs inspire others to become achievers.

Memoirs from the HillTop — a case study

For example, my *Memoirs from the HillTop* is about my life's journey. I share experiences and stories that will inspire you as a young person, giving you insights into how life was like as a young person for the average grandparent and older parent of today through my lenses. For those of us who grew up and schooled in Ghana in the 1950s, 1960s and 1970s, the book will evoke nostalgic memories and transport you back to times and events you may have forgotten about. The comments and telephone calls that have kept coming in from readers, home and abroad, bear testimony to this.

A theme that runs through the book is my conviction that there are no coincidences in life. Our steps are ordered by the Lord.

The book shares a lot of memories, in line with my belief that life is made of memories and that memories affect the quality of our lives. Subsequent to the release of the book, I have found out, to my great delight, that many of my readers have found a connection with the stories, experiences and lessons I have shared and indicated how blessed they had been as a result. Others have expressed regret for not having encountered the book earlier as they would have been saved from some mistakes and learned valuable lessons earlier in life.

An illustrative message

At this point, let me share just one of the numerous messages that have come in on my *Memoirs from the HillTop*. It is from the late Millison Narh, who was First Deputy Governor at the Bank of Ghana from 2009 to 2017. I remember meeting him at Transitions Funeral Home in Accra and the joy he exuded on telling me that he had read my Memoirs. He then followed up with the following testimonial:

"I am done with reading *Memoirs from the HillTop*, authored by Kofi Otutu Adu Labi. What a book! I must say it is an amazing book. Please if you don't have the time, don't start reading it. You may not be able to put it down even for a mundane thing as sipping your tea. It took me two and a half days to finish reading the 383-page book because it is very engaging. This book should have been available for me to read before I turned 20. It would have changed my life completely. So by implication, this book must be shared with the youth for all that it is worth.

"This book is written in simple English and is easy to understand as well as being reader friendly. The title of the book aptly describes the level the writer started his career from and never looked back. From acting head of the Legal Department of the erstwhile SSB Bank right from its inception in 1976 as a very young lawyer, to substantive Head and upwards he went in ascending the organisational ladder. Having attained an Executive position in the bank he moved on to the Central Bank, leveraging the huge social capital that he had developed over the course of his work.

"The heights that the author attained in life started from the narrative surrounding his birth.

"He was born on no other day than Easter (Good) Friday. Everybody knows the significance of the day on the Christian calendar. And true to the day of his birth, he grew up to be a pillar in the House of God. His life was characterised by regular Bible reading, prayer, and thanksgiving as well as song ministration.

"Consequently, he had the power gifts and could command a malfunctioning vehicle to receive 'life' when he went out sightseeing with his host in far-away Brazil and the vehicle brought them back home safely. This saved his host from embarrassment. Can you imagine what he (host) would have done in an era without mobile phones?

"His success in his working life was predicated on his strong communication skills. This, he acquired through copious reading of any material that came his way while growing up. This made him so confident to approach any issue that he had to deal with. And all through his working life, he related with top executives and it is therefore not surprising that he aptly titled the book *Memoirs from the HillTop*.

"The author has developed and maintained a huge high social network and many of the successes he has achieved in life have mainly been on account of this social capital. The returns on this capital have been impressive. These facilitated his work at SSB now Societe Generale Ghana, paved the way for him to pursue an MBA in Bradford and his employment at the Bank of Ghana. The goodwill borne out of his social network facilitated the solicitation for funds to build a Youth Resource Centre in his hometown, Abiriw, as well as a historic meeting with Queen Elizabeth of the United Kingdom at Buckingham Palace, to name but a few.

"His work at the Bank of Ghana, from the pinnacle of the organisation, shed light on intricacies of the Central Bank. Through the many projects he was involved in and directed, he soon gained confidence in the operations of the Bank. There is so much to learn from *Memoirs from the HillTop* and it is my hope that young professionals, in particular, will read it to help in their self-development process. To top it all, the book is also a lot of fun at various points."

Millison Narh
First Deputy Governor (retired)
Bank of Ghana

What can I say? This is what I call the writer's glow. Thank you very much, Mr Narh. May your beautiful soul continue to rest in peace.

The role of cheerleaders

Ironically, *Memoirs from the HillTop* may never have been written, were it not for the prodding and encouragement of a number of people. On my part, I felt some hesitancy in sharing my personal story, thinking that there might not be much in it for the benefit of others. Even more was a fear that no one would be interested in reading what I would share.

I was mistaken. For a number of years, some friends and associates, and even people I did not know (but who had been following my writings), kept urging me to share my life story.

My decision moment came when the internationally acclaimed medical doctor and scientist, Professor Felix Konotey-Ahulu (who died in May 2025) publicly encouraged me on two occasions (on Facebook) to write my Memoirs. That was it!

Summary of lessons from *Memoirs from the HillTop*

- Cherish the moment.
- Don't wait till tomorrow.
- Be thankful.
- Open your eyes wide. In Ghana, we say "shine your eyes."
- Count your blessings.
- Life is made of memories.
- Build pleasant memories.
- Whatever you hand finds to do, do it well, and seek to be a blessing to others.

- Live for God and love His ways.
- Do all the above, and more, and you will find fulfilment in life.

9

THE ENEMY CALLED PROCRASTINATION

"God has promised forgiveness to your repentance, but He has not promised tomorrow to your procrastination."
– St. Augustine of Hippo

The enemies standing in the way of your writing ambition, especially procrastination, have to be identified and confronted directly.

The big enemy to writing is procrastination

The inspiration to write which builds up in your mind and keeps you dreaming about and imagining the book or piece of writing you have in mind needs to be translated into reality. Sadly however, many do not cross the threshold to the finished product.

Why is this the case? One word sums it all up. That word is procrastination. Procrastination is one of the most dangerous words in the world and is the killer of dreams, projects and futures. Is it any wonder then that procrastination has been called the thief of time? Certainly not.

Many people with great ideas for stories, magazine articles, novels and plays as well as for their lives have unfortunately not been able to get to their intended destinations as a result of procrastination. When they think about the effort and time they see as required to invest in writing, they begin to experience fear and doubt. They tell themselves that tomorrow will be a better time to work on their projects. The truth however is that tomorrow never comes! Again, tomorrow is one of the most dangerous words in the world as it is one thing that kills and buries good plans and intentions.

Writer's block

My dear friend, be on the alert and start with that single line and a few paragraphs. Be on the lookout for what has become known as the Writer's block. Writer's block is a situation in which many often find themselves which prevents them from continuing to write. It can lead to the forgetting of what the prospective writer is planning to put down or even a complete slowdown or slump. It can manifest in various other ways including a feeling of inadequacy, being overwhelmed or just feeling burnt out and suddenly unable to form even simple sentences. Writer's block is a killer of many a writer's dream. One pertinent observation I have made over the years is that unless you do what you have to do and get writing, you will always find ways to avoid writing. If you do not deal with this, you might find yourself stuffing what you have written into drawers and cupboards, never to be retrieved.

Practical ways of dealing with procrastination

Tomorrow will be a good time to deal with this writing project, you may find yourself thinking aloud. The coming weekend looks like a perfect opportunity to see to it. There will be a more opportune time then, you may hear yourself saying. The reality is that tomorrow never comes and the weekend will invariably arrive with its own set of demands on your time. This has become a vicious cycle which has kept potential writers from achieving their writing dreams.

The Romans of old had a word for this phenomenon, procrastinatus. "Pro" meaning "forward" and "crastinus" signifying "of tomorrow." Over time this expression got transformed into the word procrastinate which represents the act of intentionally putting off something that should be done, with the excuse that there will be ample time and opportunity to take action later.

"Procrastination is the thief of time" is a well-known aphorism, as already stated.

The nature of the beast

- An array of undone tasks, large and small.
- The de-cluttering you keep putting off. Think of all the things, especially personal clothing

that you may not have used for years and don't even remember exist as they are buried in wardrobes and suitcases.

- An enemy. Yes, procrastination is the enemy of progress, keeping you away from seeing your dream of becoming a writer.
- Not finishing what you may even have started.
- Talking about what you are going to do without corresponding action.
- Using time and precious energy to work on never-ending household chores which can suck your productive times.

Procrastination is common for the simple reason that writing that first draft can be hard and even plain intimidating. The fact is that there is an in-built tendency with all of us which wants to postpone things our minds perceive to be hard to accomplish. We often tell ourselves that there will be a better time and opportunity to tackle the task. However, as already pointed out, this better time and opportunity may never arrive with procrastination, as tomorrow is always a moving target.

You may find yourself sitting down to watch an interesting movie on television, checking your WhatsApp or text messages, emails and social media pages. By the time you think you are ready to work on your first sentence, paragraph or page, the hours would have gone by and you will no longer be in the mood to write, whether in long hand or on your computer or telephone. Be alert to this and make a conscious effort to sit at your desk or before your computer and not rise till you have put something down.

Challenging as procrastination is, years of experience in my own work and helping other writers with theirs has taught me not to surrender to despair. Delay can be defeated.

The first step is to acknowledge that everyone procrastinates.

All of us face tasks we would rather avoid. The way out of that time and dream killer is to be vigilant to recognise "legitimate" time wasters to free you from focusing on the weightier matters confronting you.

Know tomorrow's task today

I have made it a habit to list, in order of priority, the tasks I need to work on the following day before retiring to bed. One of the things I have picked up from the School of Life is that it makes a huge difference to your morale when you know what you will be waking up to.

I feel better knowing that I am settled on what I will be doing tomorrow. For me I find that the act of writing things down helps me to remember to follow up on them. It is reassuring and calming. It brings order into the management of my time.

Eliminate piles

Do not allow files and papers to pile up on your desk. Throw away papers that are of no historical value. You will save yourself a lot of misery if you take this advice in good faith. For one thing, you will not have to waste precious hours each time you are looking for something needed for use in your writing.

10

READING AND WRITING ARE INSEPARABLE

"The greatest part of a writer's time is spent in reading, in order to write. A man will turn over half a library to make one book."
– Samuel Johnson

In seeking to be a writer, you will do well to pay attention to proven methods which have contributed to the success of other writers. That way, you will not have to reinvent the wheel.

Reading and writing are bedfellows

Writing serves to promote a reading culture. Without readers, there will be no point spending time, sleepless nights, energy and financial resources to produce books. The simple truth is that if you want to be a writer, you must read a lot and write a lot.

Now, more than ever, books have become accessible and even cheaper. The different formats of a book—hardcover, paperback, digital and audiobook—have also made reading easier and more varied. But how much time do we actually spend reading a book? When was the last time you read a book? This is a question I often ask people I meet gently as a way of encouraging them to read. Cultivating a habit of reading regularly is too good an opportunity to miss.

Reading enriches you mentally and helps keep your brain working at peak levels. Here I am collectively referring to reading good books, high quality magazines and journals with well-researched information.

Reasons to cultivate a reading habit

1. Higher emotional intelligence

Reading helps you empathise with all the different kinds of people you follow in their adventures and challenges. A lot of them experience feelings you have already experienced, and that helps you put yourself in their place. It also makes them more willing to explore what you have on offer through your writing.

2. A better vocabulary

The more you read, the more vocabulary you will learn. Such an increase in vocabulary is an asset that will enhance your value on a personal, academic, and professional level.

3. General knowledge about the world and culture.

This happens whether you read a non-fiction book or a fictional story. By reading, you get access to a lot of information that can be useful and interesting for yourself and those dear to you.

4. Better spelling

The more times you see a word written, the more easily you will remember how to spell it. This outcome comes through reading.

5. Better punctuation

I was pleased to hear a reader tell me that students should read my books to help them improve on their punctuation.

More reasons to cultivate a reading habit

1. Stress relief

Reading helps to reduce stress as the exercise helps take your mind off worrying thoughts and burdens. It can be relaxing and refreshing. It is therapeutic. I have often found myself bursting out laughing on reaching certain points in reading a book. This is a good stress reliever.

2. Critical thinking

The more you read, the more scenarios you run into and the more insights you get into how to handle them in real life situations affecting you.

3. Fun and entertainment

Reading is enjoyable. It is fun, empowering, and revealing.

Try to see each book you read as an achievement. The positive feeling you get after the achievement of finishing a book might make you want to start reading another.

Take a book with you wherever you go

This is one habit I have found very helpful in redeeming my time and in acquiring a lot of useful knowledge. Read whenever you need time alone. Connecting habits makes them stronger and makes them last longer too. If you turn your "alone time" into time for reading, you will be doing just that. Yes, reading can be a very positive experience.

11

PRACTICAL STEPS

"I find television very educating. Every time somebody turns on the set, I go into the other room and read a book." – Groucho Marx (American comedian, actor, writer, stage, film, radio and television star)

The pieces of advice in this chapter may appear pedestrian, but will prove to be a huge contributory factor to your establishing yourself as a writer. Go over them carefully.

Build a reader base

Convince the public about the value of the book. Get authentic reviews. This means getting people to make the time to read your manuscript or even the finished product and then proceeding to provide credible and unbiased reviews.

Get prospective readers excited ahead of the book release. You can do this by sharing excerpts from the book as well as some of the reviews.

Establish a strong social media presence

This should not be underrated, given the power of social media in the current dispensation.

This helps with visibility. People are more likely to buy and read a book written by an author they have some information about, however little.

You need to have a presence on social media. How are the vast majority of potential readers, the majority of whom are in the youth bracket, going to know about you if you are not known on social media? Do all that is practicable for people to get to know you and what you have on offer through your writings. I can say from experience that I have met complete strangers at places like banks and hospitals who have told me that they are familiar with my writings.

There is no gainsaying the fact that social media is powerful and has a powerful reach. Build rapport with your readers on social media by sharing some interesting content. Let the reader know about the value he or she will get from reading your book. Promote the book before launching it.

Build a personal brand

You build a personal brand while writing your content and weaving those stories into your articles and posts, whichever is applicable to you. You build your personal brand by sharing valuable content and stories from your daily life.

Keep it simple

- Don't overcomplicate things. The Bible has an interesting verse we can adopt here, "This is all that I have learnt: God made us plain and simple, but we have made ourselves very complicated" (Ecclesiastes 7:29 GNB).
- Put out content every day to grow your audience.
- Use stories to engage with your audience and build your personal brand. The truth is that people love stories and you keep them engaged when you employ that channel for your writing.

Without readers there will be no point in writing. Write so people will read and enjoy the benefits of reading.

Make sure your book creates value for readers.

The role of marketing

Leverage interactions at various gatherings—church, old school groups, children's schools, community events. I have found social interactions boosters for promoting awareness and sales of my books.

What did C. S. Lewis say about writing?

I was a voracious reader growing up and my reading got more intense during my university days. One of the authors whose books I enjoyed reading most was C. S. Lewis. Another one was P. G. Wodehouse.

When asked for advice on how to become a better writer, C. S. Lewis sent his correspondent the following list:

1. Turn off the radio.
2. Read all the good books you can, and avoid nearly all magazines.
3. Always write (and read) with the ear, not the eye. You should hear every sentence you write as if it was being read aloud or spoken. If it does not sound nice, try again.
4. Write about what really interests you, whether it is real things or imaginary things, and nothing else. (Notice this means that if you are interested only in writing, you will never be a writer, because you will have nothing to write about . . .)
5. Take great pains to be clear. Remember that though you start by knowing what you mean, the reader doesn't, and a single ill-chosen word may lead him to a total misunderstanding. In a story it is terribly easy just to forget that you have not told the reader something that he needs to know—the whole picture is so clear in your own mind that you forget that it isn't the same in his.

6. When you give up a bit of work, don't (unless it is hopelessly bad) throw it away. Put it in a drawer. It may come in useful later. Much of my best work, or what I think my best, is the rewriting of things begun and abandoned years earlier.
7. Don't use a typewriter. The noise will destroy your sense of rhythm, which still needs years of training. (Of course this advice was given before the advent of the computers we use today.)
8. Be sure you know the meaning (or meanings) of every word you use.

Turn off that radio and television!

It's important to drown out the noise always seeking our attention and representing a distraction to us from optimising our creative senses. The first thing that any serious writing activity requires is silence. This is one area of the creative and intellectual life that Lewis and his contemporaries were at a great advantage compared to us. They just had to turn off the radio. We have to turn off our phones and television screens. The reality is that we live in a noise society.

The point here is not just that quiet is necessary for the actual act of writing. Rather, quiet and its accompanying boredom, as it were, is a necessary condition for thinking carefully and deeply about anything. If you live with headphones on, always listening to music or a podcast, then you are not ever giving yourself time to just think. And if you cannot think, then you cannot write.

Devoting yourself to silence is difficult. Not only does the world hate silence—it is always trying to intrude and occupy your mind—but we hate silence too. We are a noise generation. In a sense, we are basically children looking for quick stimulation.

Just be comfortable in silence in spite of all the enticements of noise. The mornings are for quiet, thinking and reflection and you should make use of them for creativity.

We can generalise Lewis' point a bit to say that being a better writer—or engaging in any sort of intellectual, creative, or spiritual activity—involves a kind of turning away from the world. Solitude is the word to capture exactly what we need. This is not a total retreat from the world, as we still need to go on living, but rather a way of establishing boundaries. Once those boundaries are established, we can get to work on our book-writing projects.

12

WRITE YOUR RULES FOR LIVING

"We learned about honesty and integrity - that the truth matters... that you don't take shortcuts or play by your own set of rules... and success doesn't count unless you earn it fair and square." – Michelle Obama

Life has no limitations; except the ones you make. As the late Dr John Edmund Haggai put it so succinctly, self-control works best when you make your decisions ahead of time—and live according to those decisions. In effect, you are writing your Rules for Living and they come in handy when embarking on your writing journey, among other things.

According to John Edmund Haggai, it pays to live without compromise by making decisions in advance. For our context here, I want us to recommend that we should be resolute in our aspiration to become writers by not compromising on our goals. There should be no holding back. We should not allow anything to distract us from the noble task of writing we have set ourselves.

In writing about the young Jewish men taken into captivity to Babylon after the siege of Jerusalem by King Nebuchadnezzar in 605 BC, this is what John Edmund Haggai wrote: "When Daniel, Shadrach, Meshach, and Abednego were chosen for special training in Babylon, they purposed in their hearts that they would not defile themselves with the portion of the king's delicacies, nor with the wine which he drank" (Daniel 1:8).

Thus when they were actually faced with the opportunity to eat the king's food and drink the king's drink, they didn't have to make a decision under pressure. They had already made up their minds. They knew they wouldn't do it.

Self-control becomes easier when you purpose in your heart how you will act in certain situations. By application, the discipline, perseverance, single-mindedness and sense of urgency required in undertaking a writing project become easier to manage when you have made up your mind to write that book, come what may.

I know someone who checked into a hotel in an out-of-city setting for a number of weeks and only checked out after he had completed working on a manuscript that had been unduly delayed by all kinds of interruptions. He told me that the only times he stepped outside his hotel room was when he went to the restaurant for his meals. This is a perfect example of deciding how to behave in advance in line with a previously decided course of action.

Self-control works best when you make your decisions ahead of time — and live according to those decisions. In effect, you are writing your rules for living. Writing and internalising such rules not only strengthens your resolve, but also gives you greater self-confidence and serenity. Having the power of habit on your side confers great advantage.

My Personal Mission Statement

Written at the Haggai Institute for Advanced Leadership (now Haggai International) on the island of Maui, Hawaii, United States of America on 5th August, 2008:

1. To be faithful in the little things, knowing that God honours such faithfulness with big opportunities.
2. To be a diligent and ethical investor so as to be able to sow into the Kingdom of God (and give a solid education to my two youngest children).
3. To be an example of diligence and integrity in my workplace.
4. To be a man whose word can be trusted.
5. To leave a legacy of faithfulness and trust in God with my children and children's children.
6. To live a life of contentment and daily gratitude to God, believing that He knows what is best for me.

7. I believe that Christianity is a way of life and that every aspect of my life should reflect my faith.
8. To remember my humble background and through encouragement and financial support, where necessary, assist selected young people with a heart to learn and who are well behaved to develop their full potential.
9. To reduce my talks, sermons, life experiences and lessons into writing for the elevation and guidance of the present and future generations.

You need your own Personal Mission Statement to guide you along the way. It will serve as added inspiration for you on your writing journey.

13

THE NEXT STEPS

"The idea is to write it so that people hear it and it slides through the brain and goes straight to the heart." — Maya Angelou

The point about a Guide of this nature is to give an opportunity to the budding writer to put into practice what is being passed on. The excitement is to follow up, and run, with the learning points.

So let me ask you a question, when are you going to write that book you have been dreaming about as well as talking about? Well has it been said that the best time to plant a tree is 100 years ago. The same saying could well apply to your writing that book which should have happened long ago. Fortunately, all is not lost. Indeed, there is hope for there is also a saying, in answer to the question about what the best time to plant a tree is that, "The next best time is today."

So, sit down as you complete your reading of this book and start writing or punching away on your computer or tablet. Keep at it, never flagging in zeal, applying the guidelines advocated in this book and it will surprise you how far you would have got to in another six to twelve months. You have nothing to lose, and everything to gain, by following this advice. So pick up the proverbial pen and start your own writing journey. You have pontificated and strategised long enough. Now is the time for action.

In sum, finish what you start. Motivate yourself by constantly reminding yourself of the writing project that has kept you excited and sustain the momentum, drawing on the lessons you have picked along the way reading this book. The process could be painful and backbreaking, but you dare not give up. Finishing is the name of the game and a crown of joy awaits you.

What about the physical or digital book?

The proof of the pudding is in the eating, as the English would say.

Where does the actual book, physical, soft or audio come in after you have gone through all the lessons in our Guidebook? Please don't panic. Once you get to this stage, the groundwork has been laid for take-off.

There are processes you will need to complete before you see the book and experience the thrill of holding it in your hands or seeing it in soft copy or listening to it in audiobook.

These processes are fairly pedestrian but important and I would urge you to work with a Publisher, Editor or a friend familiar with book publishing to complete the process. While not going into the details here as that would be overstretching the remit of this book, let me give you the Checklist to make things easy for you.

1. Recruit a few trusted family members and friends who will be prepared to make the time to read over what you have written. They often give invaluable comments and suggestions.
2. Get an Editor to go over your manuscript. It is not for nothing that they are called Editors. I have benefitted immensely from editorial comments from my Editor friends.
3. Hand over the manuscript to a Publisher to take the manuscript through all processes leading to the printing and release of the manuscript into a book.
4. If you prefer to do self-publishing, there is nothing wrong with choosing that route.
5. Producing a book is not about printing, as some erroneously think. The Printer will only print what you give him without any value addition.
6. It is critical to have your manuscript go through standard quality assurance processes including proofreading, page layout and formatting.

7. Get a cover design that will capture the essence of the book and make it attractive.

14

TEMPLATE FOR THE STRUCTURE OF A BOOK

"If you don't know where you are going, any road will get you there." — Lewis Carroll

The following is recommended as a template to guide you as you start writing your book. I have found the structure to be useful and from all indications it has also proved to be helpful to the reader who may wish to skim through the book first before settling down to read it.

Book Cover

It is common to hear it said that one should not judge a book by its cover. The truth, however, is that a good and attractive book cover is always a plus to the patronage of a book. After all, the cover is the first thing a potential buyer and reader sees.

You should therefore get a well-thought-out and designed book cover.

Title Page

The title of your book should give a solid indication of the tone of your book.

Copyright Page

In an era in which some people are quick to plagiarise the works of others, it is important to have your book copyrighted. Your Publisher is the best person to help with the appropriate Copyright wording.

Endorsements

Statements of endorsements or praise—by people who would have read the manuscript ahead of publication. These can be helpful in giving the book credibility.

Dedication

It is customary to dedicate your work to someone or some people as a token of love, remembrance or gratitude.

Acknowledgements

A book almost always benefits from various types of support, especially in the form of editorial content and on the technical side. It is proper to acknowledge such support.

Foreword

I have found the Forewords to my books very encouraging as they reinforce the messages, stories and lessons in the books. Above all, a Foreword increases the credibility of the author.

Introduction or Preface

This serves to tell the reader the motivation for the book and the core message the reader should expect from it.

The Table of Contents

The Contents Table gives the reader the mix of chapters and subjects covered in the book together with the corresponding page numbers.

The Chapters

These should be sequentially arranged so that the book follows a natural order.

Subheadings and eye breaks

It is good practice to have subheadings and eye breaks, in terms of spacing at regular points in the chapters. This makes reading easy on the eyes, resulting in pleasurable reading.

Closing chapter or epilogue

Depending on the merits of each case and the disposition of the writer, a Closing Chapter or Epilogue will be in order. This can often prove to be the impetus to action based on the takeaways from the book.

About the author

A brief biographical or autobiographical information on the author is recommended as this can serve to elicit more interest in the book. It appears that some prospective readers skim through this section first to determine the level of interest to attach to the book, based on what they learn about the author here.

Bibliography or References

This can be useful to readers who may wish to follow up on the sources from which you drew inspiration for your book.

The Back Cover

The Back Cover or synopsis also plays a key role. I can state, from experience, that prospective readers usually scan the back cover of a book before making a purchase decision. Make what you put on the back cover convincing and show the prospective buyer the value they will get from reading your book.

15

SUMMARY OF KEY POINTS

> *"I can still remember the miraculous feeling of writing a sentence, then more sentences, telling a story. The first thing I wrote was a one-page summary of Robinson Crusoe and I am so sorry I do not have it any more; it was at that moment I became an author."*
> *— Henning Mankell*

You will by now have caught on to the essence of this book, which is to help you hone your writing skills for results. Paying close attention to the summary here should reinforce everything we have discussed so far. So here you are:

1. The overall objective of this book is to dymystify the book-writing process by taking you, the reader, through practical steps to achieve success as a writer.
2. The place of writing needs to be placed in the right perspective.
3. You should be clear about the writing style to adopt for your book project.

4. You need to keep in mind the building blocks to keep you going.
5. To be a successful writer you have to know the essence of writing.
6. Writing does not take place in a vacuum.
7. Have the reader in mind for everything you write.
8. At the end of the day, what you write should elevate the reader and make the world a better place than you found it.
9. By all means share your stories and life experiences. The world is waiting to hear from you.
10. To be a good writer, be a reader. Reading and writing go together.
11. Your desire to become a writer will get nowhere unless you deal with the enemy called Procrastination.
12. Time wasters should also be identified and dealt with in your quest to become a writer.
13. Your book will become a reality when you are patient to go through the various steps and processes shared in the book from dreaming, project conception, inception and execution to publication and book release.
14. The good news is that your aspiration to become a writer is closer to realisation than you may think.
15. Go ahead and work on that book and more!

APPENDIX 1

What I have done here is to give you sample write-ups based on ordinary day-to-day experiences with missing half socks. These turned out to be a hit with readers when I first shared them on Linkedln, Facebook and on various WhatsApp pages. The purpose is to allow you to experience the joy of reading while learning some vital life lessons. I hope you enjoy them as much as I did in putting them together.

The mystery of missing socks (1)

There is a mystery relating to missing half socks which has baffled me for years. I am still struggling to unravel the mystery.

Why do the halves of my socks get missing, especially after they have gone through laundry?

If it's any comfort, I am seeing that this is an experience others have too.

I was speaking with my son-in-law Ebenezer the other day and he shared similar experiences.

If you have been in that situation before, you will appreciate the frustration that accompanies frantic efforts to locate missing half socks whose counterparts are staring you in the face.

I decided to find out if this was a phenomenon facing others and got something interesting.

The mystery of missing socks (2)

In my quest to ascertain whether the mystery of missing socks was widespread and not a figment of my imagination, I went online to check on the subject. The results I came across are very interesting, and as my daughter Akua Adubea is telling me, it appears that the phenomenon is worldwide!

What some leading scientists in the UK have done.

According to the information I gathered from my search, some leading scientists have unravelled the cause of one of life's greatest mysteries by discovering the secrets of why our socks go missing in the wash. So it's one of life's greatest mysteries!

And the research has led them to devise a mathematical formula to predict the probability of being left in a spin with odd socks after a washing load.

It has been estimated that around 84 million socks go missing around the UK every month. Wow! It is reported that some scientists have applied science to socks in a bid to discover the factors which contribute to washday blues and to quantify their findings in a mathematical formula.

Many fanciful theories have been put forward for these laundry losses, including theft by gremlins (*ofie nipa?*) while Professor Stephen Hawking once speculated they may have fallen victim to spontaneously created black holes! Did you ever?

The Sock Loss Formula

Sock loss index = (L+C)-(P x A)

The higher the figure, the higher the likelihood of losing socks.

Where:

L = Laundry size

Calculated by multiplying the number of people in the household (p) with the frequency of washes in a week (f)

C = Washing complexity

P = The positivity towards doing laundry

A = Degree of Attention

Sharing purely for fun and for further exploration by the mathematically and statistically inclined among you.

The mystery of missing socks (3)

I was pleasantly surprised by the responses that came in on what I have shared on the mystery of missing socks. The phenomenon is indeed widespread.

Find below a sampling of comments sent to me directly on the subject:

When I read your story about missing socks, I was consoled that I was not the only one with those experiences. I seem to lose half pairs anytime I use the washing machine.

Unfortunately, I wonder what "*Ofie Nipa*" wants to do with only a half-pair of socks. Hmmm!!

A whole lot of scientific and mathematical research and analysis on missing sock when there is a simple African answer, *ofie nipa*. A simple African life.

Wow, I thought I was the lonely person on earth who loses one sock of a pair during laundry even when I have diligently tied them together and have wondered for ages where they go.

Could it be a Bermuda triangle phenomenon playing with me wherever I go, I ask myself at times? I have often felt so miserably embarrassed by these mysterious disappearances that I have not mustered enough courage to disclose it to anyone, not even my wife. Now it appears that we are dealing with a universal issue, which can best be described using a mathematical algorithm. Thank you, my fellow scientists from the UK for chasing after the mundane things of life and unravelling this mystery. I must confess that I have at times worn two lonely socks under my trousers knowing few individuals would dare check matching socks on me.

The mystery of missing socks is so real, especially during my hectic days in Tokyo! I never understood how only one sock disappears. I even started putting the lonely ones in a ziplock bag, hoping their partners would turn up eventually, but some were lost forever. Honestly disturbing when you're in a hurry. Truly one of life's strangest unsolved cases. Very interesting topic.

Not only that but your thing can get lost for months and years and then you will sometimes find it at a common place that you always patronise. Thanks for sharing, sir. God bless you.

Yeah, a common occurrence. And at the end; wearing a different sock on each foot.

Very, very common in my home, too. Although I always pack the pair rolled together for my husband and sons, sometimes the half pairs manage to disappear. Weird!

I have had to wear different halves to church a few times, but of course, nobody noticed it except me.

I resolved this by simply hand-washing my socks when I bath.

Back to basics. What a simple and at the same time perfect solution to what is apparently common phenomenon!

Thank you for this.

It saved my marriage too. As my wife was increasingly frustrated by my endless grumbling in the morning that I could not find the half-pair of my socks.

The younger ones these days have a different fashion solution; they wear unmatched socks.

If I try that, I suspect my mother may rise from her grave to disown me.

The mystery of missing socks (4)

It happened to me last Sunday. In hurriedly sending my clothing to the laundry basket to enable me get to the 7 a.m. first service on time, I unknowingly dropped one of the socks. I came back from church to find the dropped unwashed one and had to look for the washed one. Fortunately my son who had taken it off the drying lines gave it to me after a frantic search.

Hahahaaa!

I know the feeling. Panic, frustration and energy sapping!

Yes, it does happen sometimes because of the way people toss their socks when they get home. Good luck for the future.

Hahahaha, thankfully I stopped having the missing socks headache when my children became old enough to do their own laundry. In my time, though, I'd always eventually find the cause of my angst (the missing sock) hidden in a pillowcase or some other laundered item capable of being a receptacle or still lying within the washing machine's crevice. Mind you, it always took a lot of searching!

Unfortunately, the frantic search sometimes happens when one is running late and it is very frustrating, especially when all you find are the other halves of other sets. Later on, you find them dirty and tucked away in previously worn shoes.

A friend of mine put it this way... Does that one-legged monster live in your house as well?

This experience is very unpleasant.

The mystery of missing socks (5)

For women we have to find the other half of a pair of earrings as well. Having only one piece is so frustrating.

Imagine looking out for a pair of gloves, spectacle lenses for the two eyes and others that come in twos.

A hard lesson in marriage as well.

I took the role of my husband for granted until he travelled out of the country for work. I couldn't believe how disorganised I was. Simple tasks like closing security doors late at night and getting them opened in the morning, dropping off the kids at school and the fact that all four kids can call the name Mummy more than 20 times each morning to ask questions and search for their stuff in a bid to get ready to school.

Ooww, how we take the pair of socks for granted until one-half is missing . . .

Adding on to the causes, these are some more possibilities.

Oh, sometimes it's been carelessly kicked under the bed, or the kids fail to empty their bags properly when they get home, left under the car seat after freeing their feet after hours of imprisonment in sometimes tight footwear, or more seriously, they are left behind in school, gone forever!!! Because the lot to be washed are similar, sometimes no auditing is done to be sure they are all full sets.

I personally haven't experienced the missing half socks many times but mine is the missing half of my earrings. I am always losing half of my earrings and I never find them. It irritates me a lot. I keep the other half for so long hoping the other will somehow show up. After many months, I have to let the other half go. The other day, I was thinking if wearing unmatched earrings will be a new fashion statement for me.

The mystery of missing socks (6)

From Alabama, USA

I am part Irish. I think it is a leprechaun that hides a sock.

From Virginia, USA

I called them 'orphans', kept them separate till reunited with the other half! Made it a project in a household I stayed with, and the success rate will be worth documenting!! I may have to come up with the ratio soon enough so I made it a task to find orphan sock pair in a household with a male child. We had a drawer for underwear, socks, night wear, T-shirts and other miscellaneous items. Shorts were also in another drawer but trousers and shirts were hanged in the wardrobe together with jackets.

We kept the orphan socks in a transparent large ziploc bag for ease of identification. In a space of two weeks about 6 pairs out of 13 orphan half-pairs were reunited.

From Ghana

These socks issue again ooo! I can't stop laughing. If the theory of *ofie nipa* holds, then every household has them including atheist Russia and communist China.

A doctor in Ghana

I have found a good use for my single socks. I wear them unpaired for my morning walks and workouts. Nothing goes wasted. Thanks for sharing.

A doctor in the northern part of Ghana

One missing pair of socks is common. Sometimes the same colour of socks with different designs are worn.

Thinking of checking the socks of close friends to check how many of them have missing socks.

A lawyer in Ghana

Hmm, this missing socks saga. Thanks for sharing and giving me something to laugh about before going to court.

Have a very pleasant day.

From Ghana

I am very particular about my socks. I pack them in pairs and fold them so that they don't go missing but somehow I still find some missing.

APPENDIX 2

Sample statements of praise on my earlier books.

Stories to Warm Your Heart is a must-read!! Kofi Adu Labi carries you along with captivating stories told with such sincerity that you are immersed in the sheer joy of sharing his memories.

Dr Joyce R. Aryee
Management & Communications Consultant
(OVC, FIPR, FGIM, Fcia, FGHIE)

Pearls of Wisdom is an important instalment in Kofi Adu Labi's passionate, humble commitment to making a difference to this world.

Kojo Bentsi-Enchill
Senior Partner, Bentsi-Enchill, Letsa & Ankomah

It will not be enough to read through *Nuggets for Victorious Living*. For every day, take some time to think through the main thought, and then share the beauty of that day's nugget with someone. You will be doubly blessed.

Richard Crabbe
The World Bank
Formerly General Manager, African Christian Press

One cannot read this book, *They Touched us for Good* and remain the same.

If I were the head of any school or institution of leadership, I would make this book a required textbook.

David Hammond
Former General Secretary, Bible Society of Ghana and
Former Area Secretary for Africa, United Bible Societies

In the valleys of life which we all go through from time to time, a daily dose of *Wisdom, Faith and a Song* will surely buoy up the human spirit.

Dr Patience W. Stephens,
Former Director and Special Adviser on Education at the
United Nations Entity for Gender Equality and the Empowerment of Women (UN Women), New York

Kofi Adu Labi has established himself as a gifted raconteur giving perspective, ambiance and insight into a potpourri of events, occasions and personalities.

All Things Bright and Beautiful is educative, exhilarating and interesting. As its title depicts, the events recounted put a smile on your face and help you to remember pleasant memories of your own.

Andrew Kwabena Asamoah
Lawyer, former Director and Special Adviser, WHO, Geneva and Executive Chairman, A & C Development Co. Ltd.

Kofi Otutu Adu Labi continues to enrich the literature landscape of Ghana with his inimitable and felicitous writing style. His books are simple, easy to read and his messages direct and piercing.

So, it is no wonder that *Musings from the Hilltop* follows that style of simplicity, lucidity and clarity of message.

I warmly commend the book to the widest readership.

Albert K. Fiadjoe, FGA
Emeritus Professor of Public Law
Formerly, Dean of the Faculty of Law
University of the West Indies
Chairman, Constitution Review Commission, Ghana

The author's description of the ups and downs of DO's life showing his rise from a potential illiterate farmer which his father wanted him to be, to a famous academic, emphasises the importance of perseverance, determination and above all, trusting in God in all we do.

I highly recommend this book (*Crossing the Bar, The Story of Daniel Opong Amoafo*) to all.

Brig. General Dan Frimpong (Rtd)
Former CEO, African Peace Support Trainers Association (APSTA) Nairobi, Kenya
Council Chairman, Family Health University College
Teshie, Accra, Ghana

A deeply captivating memoir, with its share of humour and practical wisdom, Kofi Adu Labi writes with unguarded passion about his fascinating journey from a boy to a man; from the small village of Abiriw to Buckingham Palace; from standing on the streets waving at a passing Queen in Ghana to a personal encounter with the Queen 50 years later; and from nothing to success to significance.

Witty and constantly entertaining, *Memoirs from the HillTop* is one of those books you regret having to finish. It is lucid and joyously readable.

Kimathi Kuenyehia
Vice-Chair, International Bar Association
African Regional Forum

In *Conversations from the HillTop*, I have been given a glimpse of the history of Ghana—its past, its present and its future. A combination of people, place, story and memory which open a window for me on Ghana's story. From my perspective, living in the UK, it is exciting to read Kofi's exhortation to Ghana's writers—'your story is waiting to be written' and the challenge to liberate Ghana from the narrative of foreigners, as Ghana tells its own story. *Conversations from the HillTop* is surely a contribution from Kofi Adu Labi to Ghana, telling its own story. I want to hear more. The West needs to hear more.

Sandra Mary Rome
Retired Director of Children's Services
Spurgeons Children's Charity
Somerset, United Kingdom

I was blessed reading *Timeless Wisdom from the HillTop*. As the title suggests, the book is filled with wisdom and—although borne out of the disruption of the COVID-19 pandemic—its lessons are both timely and timeless.

I found *Timeless Wisdom from the HillTop* to be practical and inspiring. It is a valuable resource for Christians of all ages seeking to strengthen and enrich their own walk with God.

Joan Campbell
South African author and MAI-Africa Trustee

I would have titled it "A manual of Life" but if there ever was an apt title for this book, *Counsels from the HillTop* must be it. This is an extremely powerful and remarkable book by a truly outstanding and knowledgeable individual. Kofi Adu Labi "descends" from the HillTop and skilfully uses his deep knowledge and experience to counsel the old and the young alike on life's imperatives. The book is littered with nuggets of wisdom that everybody, particularly the youth, would benefit from immensely. The remarkable thing is that paragraph after paragraph, chapter after chapter, one is left thinking, "That was blindingly obvious and common-sense". But alas, as we all know, common sense is anything but common!

Kodwo Osafo Binfoh (FCCA, MBA)
Former Head of Finance, Long Term Investment Programme,
National Air Traffic Services Ltd
United Kingdom

This book brings to the fore the essence of purposeful living and draws attention to all stages of life for any person who desires to have a fulfilling life.

I have been pleasantly educated by reading *Living With Purpose — HillTop Perspectives*. May it be widely read by the young and the old for the good of humanity and posterity.

Prof. Dora Francisca Edu-Buandoh

Former Pro-Vice Chancellor
University of Cape Coast, Ghana and
Lay Chair of Evangelical Methodist Church of Christ, Ghana
Now High Commissioner of Ghana to Canada

In a world often marked by confusion and moral ambiguity,

Gems from the HillTop provides clarity and direction, urging its readers to rise above mediocrity and distractions, and to live with intentionality, faith, and integrity.

May this book inspire you to live fully and reflect God's love and grace in all that you do. Profound blessings to all who embark on this enriching journey.

Sidney Lino de Oliveira, PhD
Business Administration
Professor, PUC Minas - Brazil

Elder Kofi gives us rich anecdotes on what it means to be an Investor, not a Taker. By using stories and examples from scripture and the lives of people, we get challenged to think beyond ourselves to impact the lives of others. One question readers should ask themselves is what kind of legacy they want to be remembered for.

Let us be deliberate in making a difference during our time on earth. As a word of advice, every reader should have a pen and paper next as he or she reads this book, *Become an Investor! Not a Taker – HillTop Secrets*. There are riches in there that need to be captured.

Alex Njukia
Senior Technical Advisor
World Vision East Africa
and Lay Pastor, International Christian Centre—
Imara, Nairobi, Kenya

BIBLIOGRAPHY

Adu Labi, K. O. (2016a). *Pearls of wisdom.* Step Publishers.

Adu Labi, K. O. (2016b). *Stories to warm your heart.* Step Publishers.

Adu Labi, K. O. (2021). *Memoirs from the hilltop.* Digibooks.

Adu Labi, K. O. (2024). *Become an investor! Not a taker – HillTop secrets.* Step Publishers.

Andah, C., & Baraka, Z. (2023). *Letters of hope to my younger self.* Triple A Press.

Chambers, O. (1963). *My utmost for his highest.* Discovery House Publishers.

Darmani, L. (2019). *All the way to Calvary.* Step Publishers.

Foster, R. J. (2018). *Celebration of discipline.* HarperOne.

Frimpong, D. K. (2023). *The military my life.* Digibooks.

Gibbs, J., & Mapanje, J. (Eds.). (1999). *The African writers' handbook.* African Books Collective Ltd.

Gyan-Apenteng, N. K. (2025). *What I choose to remember.* Digibooks.

Haggai, J. E. (1989). *Be careful what you call impossible*. Harvest House Publishers.
Nightingale, E. (2005). *The strangest secret*. Simple Truths.

THE AUTHOR

Kofi Otutu Adu Labi is a lawyer, management consultant and author. He is also a Church Elder, teacher and preacher.

He was educated at Ofori Panin Secondary School, Achimota School, University of Ghana, the Ghana School of Law and the University of Bradford School of Management. He was called to the Ghana Bar on 2nd October, 1975.

He also studied at the International Law Institute (Washington DC), the Cranfield School of Management and London Business School. He is an alumnus of the Haggai Institute for Advanced Leadership, Hawaii.

He served as Advisor under two Governors of the Bank of Ghana (Dr Paul Acquah and Mr Kwesi Amissah-Arthur). He started his banking career at the then SSB Bank (now Societé Generale Ghana) as a pioneering staff in 1976 and was the founding head of the Legal Department, before rising to the position of General Manager.

He is a Director of the Ghana Institute of Linguistics, Literacy and Bible Translation (GILLBT). He has held a number of directorships including Commissioner, Securities and Exchange Commission Ghana, the National Pensions Regulatory Authority, Taysec Construction, Taysec Properties, Scripture Union Ghana, Victory Presbyterian Church School and the Bible Society of Ghana. He is a member of the Projects and Investments Committee of the Presbyterian Church of Ghana. He had before then served as a Trustee of the Presbyterian Church of Ghana Education Foundation for over 10 years. He has been a Member of Council of the Christian Service University, Kumasi. He is a Trustee of the Esther Ocloo Memorial Foundation. He has held the position of Senior Presbyter and Presbyter at the Dansoman Emmanuel and Victory (Fafraha) congregations of the Presbyterian Church of Ghana respectively.

In June 2010, he was the guest of Queen Elizabeth at the Royal Tea Tent as part of the Queen's annual tea parties.

In March 2011 he was invited to speak on a panel at the first-ever Financial Infrastructure conference of the World Bank in Rio de Janeiro, Brazil. He spoke on the topic: "The role of Central Banks in a secured transactions reform programme."

In May of the same year, the International Finance Corporation (IFC) invited him to attend the Fourth United Nations Conference on the Least Developed Countries (LDC-IV) in Istanbul as a panelist. The purpose of the Conference was to adopt new measures and strategies for the sustainable development of the LDCs into the next decade.

He has served as a member of the Advisory Board of the Ghana Association of Writers (GAW). This is his 17th book, having written sixteen other books of which seven have so far been endorsed by the National Council for Curriculum and Assessment (NaCCA) as supplementary readers for schools in Ghana. He has also contributed a chapter to another book, *Letters of Hope to my Younger Self*. He is a recipient of the GAW Achievement Award, 2019.

He has been married to Elioenai since 1978 and they have five adult children and three grandchildren.

Printed in Dunstable, United Kingdom

80750352R00070